U.S. BATTLESHIPS

in action
Part 2

by Rob Stern
illustrated by Don Greer

line drawings by Kevin Wornkey

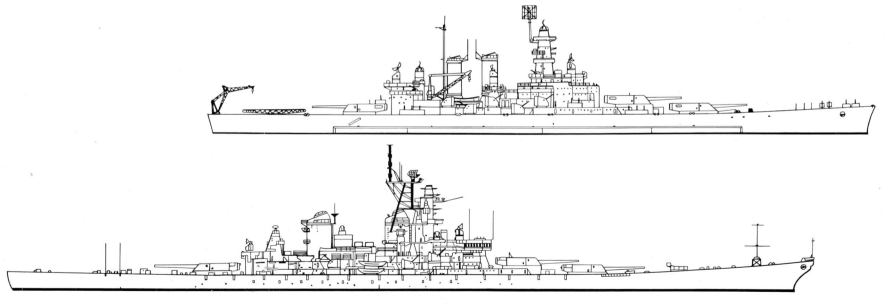

squadron/signal publications

Warships No. 4

Turning at high speed, South Dakota spouts the smoke of the deadly AA fire that claimed twenty-six victims during the Battle of Santa Cruz, 26 October 1942. Scheme is Measure 22.

Camouflage

Measure 1 — Dark Gray System (January 1941): Dark Gray (5-D) on all vertical surfaces up to the level of the funnel tops, Light Gray (5-L) on all higher vertical surfaces.

Measure 5 — Painted Bow Wave (January 1941): upper edge of false wave in white, filled in with Dark Gray (5-D).

Measure 11 — Sea Blue System (September 1941): Sea Blue (5-S) on all vertical surfaces.

Measure 12 — Graded System (September 1941): Sea Blue (5-S) up to level of main deck, Ocean Gray (5-0) up to level of top of superstructure, Haze Gray (5-H) above.

Measure 12 — Graded System (Modified): Sea Blue (5-S), Ocean Gray (5-O), Haze Gray (5-H), as above, but with a wavy edge between colors and splotching for a more blended effect.

Measure 15 — Disruption System (June 1942): wavy disruptive pattern generally employing Navy Blue (5-N), Ocean Gray (5-O) and Haze Gray (5-H).

Measure 21 — Navy Blue System (June 1942): Navy Blue (5-N) on all vertical surfaces.

Measure 22 — Graded System (June 1942): Navy Blue (5-N) up to level of lowest point of main deck, upper edge horizontal, remaining vertical surfaces Haze Gray (5-H).

Measure 31 — Dark Pattern System (March 1943): disruptive pattern generally employing Dull Black (Bk), Ocean Gray (5-0) and Haze Gray (5-H).

Measure 32 — Medium Pattern System (March 1943): disruptive pattern generally employing Dull Black (Bk), Ocean Gray (5-0) and Light Gray (5-L).

Measure 33 — Light Pattern System (March 1943): disruptive pattern generally employing Navy Blue (5-N), Haze Gray (5-H) and Pale Gray (5-P).

Note: There also existed a more rarely used **Measure 31a** which substituted Navy Blue (5-N) for Dull Black (Bk), giving a scheme similar in overall effect to Ms. 32.

If you have any photographs of the aircraft, armor, soldiers or ships of any nation, particularly wartime snapshots, why not share them with us and help make Squadron/Signal's books all the more interesting and complete in the future. Any photograph sent to us will be copied and the original returned. The donor will be fully credited for any photos used. Please indicate if you wish us not to return the photos. Please send them to: Squadron/Signal Publications, Inc., 1115 Crowley Dr., Carrollton, TX 75011-5010.

Acknowledgements

I would again like to thank those people who have assisted me in putting this book together. Jim Sullivan and Jerry Goldstein lent photos from their collections which filled important holes in this work. LCdr George Farrar supplied the photos of Iowa's recent travels. In particular, I would like to thank Chief Gene Romano of the Navy's Dallas Navy Information Office who was unfailingly helpful every time I called on him.

Abbreviations

AA — Anti-Aircraft

CIWS — Close-In Weapons System

DP — Dual Purpose, referring to weapons used against both surface and air targets and to their directors.

ESM — Electronic Support Measures

TF — Task Force

TG — Task Force

Wreathed by black puffs of her own AA fire, South Dakota maneuvers at high speed during the Battle of Santa Cruz, 26 October 1942. Part of Enterprise's screen, South Dakota brought down 26 attackers during the action, a record that still stands for one ship on one day. Significantly, Enterprise escaped serious damage that day while Hornet, which lacked fast battleship protection, was sunk. Whether or not there was a direct connection, Pacific Fleet staff drew the easy conclusion, condemning the fast battleships to be little more than AA escorts for fast carriers during the rest of the war. (USN/NARS)

INTRODUCTION

Fast Battleships in World War II and Beyond

The Washington Treaty of 1922 brought a halt to an ambitious program of capital ship construction by the US Navy. Seven battleships and six battlecruisers were either broken up during construction or never started. One battleship, USS Washington (BB-47), was 75.9 per cent complete when work was abandoned on 8 February 1922. The treaty limited the United States Navy and Great Britain's Royal Navy to eighteen and twenty capital ships respectively, Japan to ten and France and Italy to fewer yet. In the decade that followed the signing of the treaty only two new battleships were completed, the Royal Navy's Nelson and Rodney which had been started in 1922 and were specifically permitted by the Washington Treaty because of the obsolescence of many of the RN's existing capital ships. Otherwise, there followed a 'holiday' in battleship construction broken only in 1932 by the laying down of France's 26,500t Dunkirque.

The US Navy accepted the Washington Treaty's limitations with mixed emotions. Line admirals hated to lose all those beautiful new battleships but the more politically attuned eventually concluded that the economic realities of the postwar world probably would have led to the cancellation of those projects anyway. As world economies boomed in the

The first action seen by fast battleships was in the Atlantic, when Washington was assigned briefly to the Royal Navy during the spring of 1942 in order to free British battleships for other operations. Washington lies at anchor at Scapa Flow with HMS Victorious after one of her two convoy protection missions before departing for the Pacific in July. (USN/NARS)

'Roaring '20s', taxpayers showed little inclination to fund massive fleets while still paying off the debt of World War One. Certainly the US Navy had little grounds for complaint about the ultimate results of the treaty. Having gone into WWI as the world's third largest navy, it was now acknowledged as being one of two naval 'superpowers', and because its ships were newer and generally better designed and built than the Royal Navy's wartime construction, most unbiased observers concluded that the treaty left the US Navy the world's strongest. Further, the war had clarified its strategic mission. The only other navy of comparable size was a close ally capable of guarding the Atlantic with little help, leaving the US Navy free to face west, toward the only remaining potential rival, Japan.

The Great Depression brought momentous changes and led to the emergence of major characters on the world stage, including Mussolini, Hitler and, in 1932, Franklin Delano Roosevelt. As an ex-Assistant Secretary of the Navy and as a Democratic president determined to use public funds to help raise the US out of the depression, FDR saw the building of new naval vessels as an essential element in his economic plans. Other parts of the fleet had been neglected far longer than the battleline, however, and the original Roosevelt construction budgets contained monies for aircraft carriers, cruisers and destroyers, but none for battleships. The surprise Japanese announcement in December 1934 that they didn't intend to renew the Washington Treaty when it expired in 1936 changed this situation dramatically. For the first time in over a decade, work began on designing new US Navy battleships.

Battleship design after the 1922 treaty had become a political question. The Royal Navy pressed hard for increasing restrictions on battleship size and armament, because the bulk of their battleline was smaller, and older. In particular, the British wanted to substantially lower the existing gun size, pressing for the imposition of a 14in limit on armament (two inches less than the treaty already specified). The US Navy was willing to accept smaller displacement limits, because of the restriction placed on the growth of US naval vessels by the Panama Canal. However, most American admirals disagreed strongly over the armament limit, not wanting to build new capital ships less powerfully armed than the existing Colorados — United States Navy (USN), Nelsons — Royal Navy (RN) or Nagatos — Imperial Japanese Navy (IJN), each carrying 16in main guns. Nevertheless, in October 1935 the US Navy agreed to the British limits with the proviso that all signers of the Washington Treaty (including Japan) must concur by 1 April 1937. Failing that, the armament limit would automatically revert to 16in.

Delaying the decision on gun size created further problems. The US had no intention of waiting until 1937 to begin designing its new battleships, yet it was impossible to create even preliminary designs without a turret size and barbette weight, both very much gun size dependent. Admiral Standley came up with a clever solution, instructing BuShips to design their new battleships with interchangeable triple 16in or quadruple 14in mounts of identical weight and size. Thus the effects of the delayed decision could be postponed, though not indefinitely. The gun size question had become an issue in the 1936 presidential campaign. The Republicans charged that FDR's publicly stated preference for the bigger gun would initiate an arms race. The American voter was unimpressed by the Republican argument and returned Roosevelt for a second term. The Japanese, fully aware that their vote was critical to the agreement and thus to the design process of the new US capital ships, delayed their announcement as long as possible. Only on 27 March 1937 did they make public their rejection of the proposed limits. (The political nature of this delay is obvious when it is noted that the final design for the 64,000ton, 18in armed Yamato class was approved that very month.)

Even with the Japanese rejection of the 14in gun limit, Roosevelt was reluctant to be the first to publicly authorize the larger gun caliber. The British had felt compelled to begin construction of their new capital ships in 1937 and had decided the year before to build their King George V class with 14in guns (over the loud protests of another ex-Navy Minister — Winston Churchill). Therefore, Roosevelt passed along to the Navy his decision in favor of the 14in main armament in April 1937. The Navy's General Board was outraged. 14in guns fired a projectile weighing about 1500lbs. A 16in shell is about 1000lb heavier. By using a stronger powder charge, a 14in shell can be fired as far and with similar destructive power as the larger shell, though not without paying a heavy price in shortened gun life. But, as the General Board pointed out in an impassioned plea sent to FDR on 17 May 1937, the real difference was in the guns' relative immune zones. (An immune zone is that band of ranges at which a particular thickness of armor will stop a shell. At shorter ranges a shell still retains enough energy to penetrate the armor belt and at longer ranges a shell would be plunging at a great enough angle to pass above the armor belt. In between these ranges lies the so-called immune zone in which protective armor is effective. Weight considerations limited the belt armor of most modern battleships to approximately 12in and deck armor to 5-6in.) The inner zone of vulnerability wasn't a major concern to the Board as both guns had similar performance at short range. However, their performance differed dramatically at long range. At long range, where most naval engagements could be expected to take place, the 14in gun suffered. Because it fired a lighter projectile at greater speed, it had a much flatter trajectory which resulted in a much smaller long range vulnerable zone for the target. The difference was significant. According to the General Board, the 14in gun provided an outer zone of only 500 yards against a typical enemy capital ship while the larger gun's outer zone was ten times wider.

FDR tried one more time to delay the decision. In early June of 1937, he had Ambassador Grew again ask the Japanese to agree to the lower limit. They responded that they would accept only on the condition that the US and Britain agree to limit the number of their capital ships to the same number (10) imposed on the IJN. This was totally unacceptable to Roosevelt and on 10 July 1937 he reversed himself and ordered the new US battleships armed with 16in guns.

Vacillation on the question of gun caliber resulted in a delay of about a month as drawings were again revised by BuShips. But once the decision to proceed had been made, construction was pressed forward with a will. The first two battleships (North Carolina and Washington) were authorized in the Fiscal Year 1938 (FY38) budget and were laid down on 27 October 1937 and 14 June 1938 respectively. Four more were budgeted in FY39, South Dakota being laid down on 5 July 1939, Massachusetts 15 days later, Indiana on 20 November 1939 and Alabama on 1 February 1940. The Iowa class was authorized in two separate batches. Two were funded in FY40, Iowa being laid down on 27 June and New Jersey on 16 September 1940. The two remaining Iowas were included in the FY41 budget and were laid down on 6 January 1941 (Missouri) and 25 January 1941 (Wisconsin).

The 'Two-Ocean Navy Bill' passed by Congress in 1940 authorized seven more battleships, which included two more Iowas (Illinois and Kentucky) and five huge Montanas that would have carried a fourth triple 16in turret and would have been too wide to pass through the Panama Canal. Both of the final Iowas were laid down and two of the Montanas were ordered but all were cancelled in 1943. Kentucky was so far advanced that her nearly completed hull was preserved on the graving slip for five more years while discussions were held as to possible uses for the hull. She was finally launched to clear the ways in 1950 and even then was retained for eight more years before she was sold for scrap in 1958.

One of the great illusions of history which many Americans unfortunately believe is the myth that the Japanese carried out their attack on the 7th of December and on the 8th of December America began building the navy that ultimately won the war. Such was obviously not the case. All ten of the fast battleships that helped win that victory had been building for at least ten months when Pearl Harbor was attacked. The North Carolinas were launched within two weeks of each other in June 1940 and were commissioned in April and May 1941. In fact, three out of the four South Dakota class were already in the water prior to the Japanese attack. The Navy that destroyed the Imperial Japanese Navy wasn't built, and couldn't have been built, in response to Pearl Harbor. Its beginnings go back six full years before Pearl Harbor. But while the Japanese attack on Pearl Harbor in

North Carolina working up in the Atlantic along with another new warship, the carrier Hornet, January 1942. Hornet departed for the Pacific before North Carolina, but they were to meet again during operations off Guadalcanal in September when the battleship formed part of Hornet's screen. (USN/NARS)

While engaged in this activity, North Carolina was hit by a single torpedo from a spread of six fired by the Japanese submarine I-19 on 14 September 1942. Three hit Wasp and sank her, and another hit the destroyer O'Brien, leading to her eventual sinking. The torpedo hit North Carolina low on her port bow, abreast No.1 turret, blowing this hole in her side plating below her armor belt. She took on a five degree list but was able to maintain her station during further high-speed maneuvers. Permanent repairs required drydocking at Pearl Harbor, 11 October 1942. (USN/NHC)

no way affected the creation of the fast battleships, it had a drastic effect on their deployment.

The mortal threat to England posed by German U-boats had caused a profound shift in the westward-looking orientation of the US fleet. During 1941, as the Navy became increasingly involved in the job of Atlantic convoy protection, the token Atlantic Fleet began to be significantly reinforced. The US Navy, along with a lot of others, underestimated the Japanese, believing that a reduced US Pacific Fleet could hold the Japanese at bay short of the Philippines while Hitler was being defeated. The North Carolinas, still working up off the east coast along with the new carrier Hornet, were to be retained indefinitely in the Atlantic. The attack on Pearl Harbor radically altered these plans. As soon as they were certified ready for combat, both battleships were sent to the Pacific to help rebuild the devasted battle line.

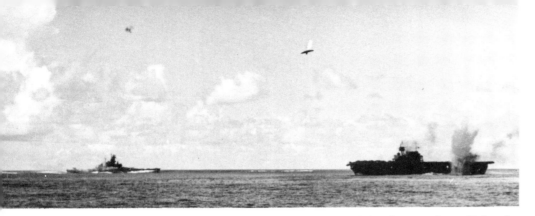

South Dakota at work at Santa Cruz, 26 October 1942. A bomb near-misses Enterprise while the Val (Aichi D3A2 Type 99 Carrier Bomber Model 12) that dropped it goes down in flames, another of the 26 victims of South Dakota's accurate AA fire that day. South Dakota took a 500lb bomb on the roof of B turret, which failed to penetrate. The explosion wounded some bridge personnel including the captain but didn't slow the ship or in any way impair her ability to fight. (USN/NARS)

(Above and Below) A pair of Zuikaku's Kates (Nakajima B5N2 Type 97 Carrier Attack Bombers Model 12) come in low on South Dakota's bow during the Battle of Santa Cruz. One of the attackers veered away sharply but the other, hit by South Dakota's AA barrage, flew a straight course over the battleship's fantail before crashing on her far side. Both torpedoes missed. (USN/NARS)

While still technically working up, Washington became the first of the fast battleships to participate in combat operations. She was sent from her base at Casco Bay to Scapa Flow along with Wasp on 25 March 1942 in order to free elements of the RN's Home Fleet for the invasion of Madagascar. At the beginning of May, she participated in a mixed force covering the passage of convoys PQ15 and QP11 to and from Murmansk. Along with King George V (KGV), Washington patrolled the straits between Iceland and Norway in case the Kriegsmarine decided to come out. In the event, there was no combat, but KGV did add a bit of excitement when she collided with one of the destroyers. Washington was sent out on patrol from Scapa one more time. On 28 June 1942, she sortied along with Duke of York to cover the ill-fated PQ17. This time the Germans responded with OPERATION ROSSELSPRUNG. Four major Kriegsmarine surface units, including Tirpitz, were moved toward Alta prior to being launched against the convoy. The cautious British recalled the escorts and dispersed the convoy. The Germans, equally fearful, never got out of Norwegian coastal waters, but they accomplished everything they could have wished by causing the dispersal of the convoy. Washington completed her Atlantic tour of duty with this operation and departed for the Pacific after a brief stop on the east coast.

North Carolina, in the company of Wasp, hadn't waited. The opening engagements of the war in the Pacific had taken a terrible toll of American carriers. By mid-May 1942, Lexington had been sunk, Saratoga had been torpedoed and Yorktown damaged. Wasp, escorted by North Carolina, was needed desperately. Before they transitted the Panama Canal on 10 June, the immediate crisis in the Pacific had passed, but with the loss of Yorktown at Midway, their immediate presence was still very much required. Wasp and North Carolina, along with four cruisers, were officially designated TF18 at San Diego on 15 June 1942 and sent on to the South Pacific. Upon arrival, North Carolina was detached from Wasp and assigned to TF61.2 guarding Enterprise, which was providing air support for the WATCHTOWER landings on Guadalcanal beginning on 7 August. As part of TG61.2, North Carolina participated in the inconclusive two-day Battle of the Eastern Solomons, 23-24 August 1942. What that battle did prove was the value of a fast battleship as an AA platform. At one point in the engagement, North Carolina became so completely enshrouded in the smoke of her own AA that Enterprise radioed to inquire if she was on fire. In one eight minute period she engaged 18 enemy aircraft and claimed seven. The implications of this performance, for better or worse, weren't lost on the Navy.

Despite this success, North Carolina wasn't available to protect Enterprise when she was next engaged because of what must be recorded as history's most successful spread of torpedoes. On 14 September, the Japanese submarine I-19 fired a salvo of six torpedoes at Wasp from a range of about 1500yd. One missed aft and continued on for over ten miles, passing under no less than two destroyers, before hitting North Carolina on her port bow under the armor belt. It tore a 32ft hole in her side plating and allowed the entry of nearly 1000 tons of sea water. Two of the torpedoes passed forward of Wasp, one of which eventually hit the destroyer O'Brien, also in port bow, after travelling 11 miles. The remaining three torpedoes hit Wasp's starboard side. The toll was terrible. Wasp was fatally wounded, O'Brien had lost her bow (causing her sinking three days later) and North Carolina took on a 5 degree list and flooded her forward magazine as a preventive measure. The toughness of these new battleships was amply demonstrated that day. Despite the significant damage, North Carolina maintained her position in Enterprise's screen and maneuvered at speeds up to twenty-five knots for the rest of the day. While never in danger of sinking, the damage was major and the next day North Carolina departed for Pearl Harbor along with Enterprise for repairs that would keep her out of action until January 1943.

The fleet in the South Pacific would be without a fast battleship for less than three weeks, because Washington arrived at Noumea from the Atlantic on 9 October 1942, and a week later South Dakota set out from Pearl Harbor with Enterprise, as part of a reconstituted TF61. Washington was assigned to TF64, along with three cruisers and six destroyers, performing escort duties for convoys running between Noumea and Guadalcanal, under the command of RAdm Willis A. 'Ching' Lee, formerly of Adm King's CinCUS staff. Lee arrived in the South Pacific to take direct command of the fast battleships, under new ComSoPac VAdm William F. 'Bill' Halsey, an assignment he would hold for most of the war. On a number of occasions Lee would miss major action by narrow margins, but he was now at the right place at the right time. Lee and TF64 were beginning the single most exciting month of the fast battleships' war, one that would culminate in their only engagement with enemy capital ships.

The month opened with the Japanese again trying to drive carrier forces down into the Solomons area. Once again US carriers were there to intervene and again a fast battleship provided escort. South Dakota, still assigned to screen Enterprise, protected the carrier from harm at the Battle of Santa Cruz, 26 October 1942, and in the process claimed a record 26 victories. The following day, Washington was near-missed by a torpedo from I-15. In a separate incident on the same day, South Dakota was also the target of a Japanese torpedo. While evading the torpedo, South Dakota collided with the destroyer Mahan. Fortunately, neither ship suffered serious damage.

Lee's battleships were back in action again two weeks later. On 11 November 1942, TF64 was reformed on South Dakota, Washington and escorting destroyers Benham and Walke and assigned to protect Enterprise's TF16. Two days later, after the disastrous First Naval Battle of Guadalcanal, TF64 strengthened by destroyers Preston and Gwin was ordered to the vicinity of Guadalcanal in case Japanese Adm Kondo tried another sortie into 'Ironbottom Sound'. It proved to be a wise precaution. As Lee approached from the east on 14 November, Kondo was coming down the 'Slot' with the battleship Kirishima, heavy cruisers Takao and Atago, light cruisers Nagara and Sendai and eight destroyers.

The forces approaching each other were fairly evenly matched, at least on paper. The Japanese had more ships but Lee had the bigger guns. Also, Lee had radar, the Japanese did not, but the Japanese had much more night fighting experience and had far superior torpedo tactics and equipment. Kondo split his force into four separate columns for their approach to Savo Is. Lee's group was in a simple line ahead, the destroyers in the lead followed by Washington and South Dakota.

Sendai's lookouts spotted the US line at 2215 on 14 November 1942, reporting it as four destroyers and two heavy cruisers. Lee's line, as yet unaware of the Japanese, turned due west at approximately 2245 in order to close the southern entrance to Ironbottom Sound. Purely by chance, this put him directly across the line of advance of three of Kondo's four columns. Finally at 2300, Washington's radar picked up Sendai east of Savo, visual contact following a few minutes later. At 2317, Washington opened fire at Sendai and her single escorting destroyer. The two Japanese turned and fled without damage. The rest of Sendai's scouting group, two destroyers, followed by the van of Kondo's bombardment force, Nagara and four more destroyers, now opened fire with devastating effect on the lead US destroyers. As the two lines raced past each other on opposite courses, the Japanese struck with gunfire and torpedoes. Preston (DD379) came under concentrated fire from Nagara at 2327 and was literally blown out of the water, sinking within nine minutes. Walke (DD416) was next in Nagara's sights and was hit by a torpedo at 2332. She broke in two at the forecastle and within 11 minutes she too was gone.

The action wasn't completely one-sided, however. As the battleships trailing the US line came into action, the tide of the battle began to swing against the Japanese. The lead enemy destroyer, Ayanami, was hit by three salvos from South Dakota at 2332, turning out of line engulfed in flames. Eight minutes later the fire reached her rear magazines, and in a spectacular explosion she became the third destroyer to sink in a span of seven minutes. The carnage was far from over. The next US destroyer in line, Gwin, was hit by 6in shells

While supporting the Torch landings off Casablanca, 8 November 1942, Massachusetts came under fire from the incomplete Jean Bart moored inside the harbor. Nine salvos were fired in reply, scoring five hits and effectively discouraging the French battleship from further rash action. (Above Right) During a lull in the action, sailors move about on Massachusetts' fantail. Note the two oversized American flags flown in the vain hope that the Vichy French wouldn't fire on their WWI allies. (USN/NHC) (Middle Right and Below Right) Jean Bart, much worse for wear after the engagement. Only one of her two quadruple 15in turrets was complete and that one was hit and knocked out during the brief fight. The damage to her bow provides ample evidence of the effectiveness of 16in gunfire. (NASM)

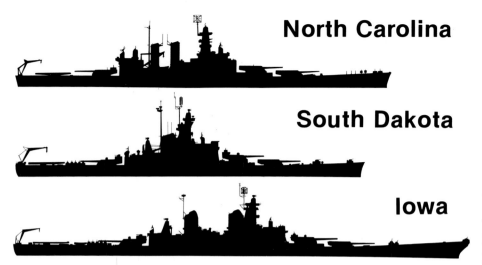

North Carolina

South Dakota

Iowa

In part because of her own success as an AA platform during the Battle of the Eastern Solomons, North Carolina and the rest of the fast battleships spent most of the war as escorts to the fast carrier groups. North Carolina is seen from Lexington during operations off Saipan, 18 June 1944. That same evening the seven fast battleships in TF58 were joined together in an ad hoc battleline (TG58.7) in preparation for the climactic battle which began the next day. (USN/NARS)

from Nagara at 2337 and forced out of line. Benham, the last US destroyer, was hit in the bow by a torpedo only a minute later. Down to five knots and taking water, she too dropped out of action.

Suddenly it was quiet. At 2343 Nagara's column pulled out of range to the east, leaving the two US battleships still steaming westward. Bearing down was the last of Kondo's columns, with Kirishima, the two heavy cruisers and two destroyers. The opening action had tipped the scales against Lee and he was further hampered by critical equipment failures. At this, the worst possible moment, South Dakota's FC fire control radar failed. Nor were Lee's problems made any easier by the fact that his two battleships were no longer in line. In order to avoid the survivors of the sinking destroyers, South Dakota had swung to the north leaving her several hundred yards closer to Kondo than Washington. Suddenly, at about 2350, South Dakota was illuminated by searchlights on Kirishima. Simultaneously a murderous fire descended from all five Japanese ships. Hit rapidly by 27 shells of 5in or larger and unable to effectively respond, with No.3 turret temporarily disabled, uncontrolled fires in her superstructure and with 58 dead and 60 wounded, South Dakota chose the prudent course and turned away to the south.

South Dakota's suffering had one positive side-effect. Washington, invisible to the Japanese behind South Dakota and with working fire control radars, had worked into perfect position to extract a measure of revenge. Opening fire at exactly midnight at a range of 8400yd, Washington hit Kirishima with nine 16in rounds and over forty 5in rounds in quick succession. Kirishima's poorly protected steering gear was disabled and she began steaming in large circles. Kondo had had enough and ordered a general retirement. Washington gave chase for a few miles but the action was over. Kirishima, unable to steer a straight course, was reluctantly abandoned and scuttled, sinking at 0320 on 15 November 1942.

For the first and only time in the war, US fast battleships met one of their opposites and they had won. But it should be noted that Kirishima was just a bit less than 30 years old at the time of her demise, making her a full two design generations older than either American she faced. She had started life as a British-designed battlecruiser of WWI vintage and had been progressively modernized until she was rated as a fast battleship. Still, her armor protection was only about 1/2 that of either American. A sister, Hiei, had been put out of action by similar damage to the steering compartment by 8in gunfire only two nights before. The Second Battle of Guadalcanal is listed as an American victory because at dawn they still held the waters over which the battle had been fought. Like many of the American victories in the Solomons, the price was high. Three US destroyers had sunk (Benham (DD397) went down later that day) and the remaining destroyer and South Dakota were damaged. While South Dakota's injuries never threatened her life, she would be out of action for seven months.

Meanwhile, other units of the South Dakota class were completing training and reporting for duty. Massachusetts was first engaged on 8 November 1942 off the coast of North Africa, where she had escorted the landing force for OPERATION TORCH. While there she accomplished the 'surgical' neutralization of the French battleship Jean Bart, which had been rash enough to fire on the landing force. Massachusetts hit Jean Bart with five 16in shells, knocking out her only operational turret. Later in the day a number of Vichy destroyers sortied. One 16in shell from Massachusetts and a number of 8in rounds from Tuscaloosa were sufficient to sink Fougeaux. During this action Massachusetts was near-missed by four torpedoes from a French submarine, one missing by only 15ft. Later a single 16in shell from Massachusetts wrecked the forward section of the destroyer Milan and put her out of action. At about 1100, Massachusetts was hit by a single 5.1in shell from the destroyer Boulonnais, which was promptly dispatched by concentrated fire from the battleship and the light cruiser Brooklyn. The sortie ended when Massachusetts put a 16in round into the Vichy light cruiser Primaquet, which was leading the flotilla. The French had fought bravely, but their light forces were no match for a fast battleship's firepower and the Vichy commander prudently headed back into harbor.

Indiana reported for duty at Tonga in late November 1942, where she supported Washington and the now repaired North Carolina in escort duties covering Enterprise and Saratoga during continuing operations off Guadalcanal. There was little action for the battleships as both sides seemed exhausted by the fierce naval battles in the Solomons. For a period of about six months starting at the beginning of 1943, there were no major battles in the South Pacific. The fast battleships spent much of that period wallowing at Noumea, with their crews passing the days hunting wild boars on New Caledonia and the nights drinking Australian champagne. Time was now very much on the side of the Americans and when the offensive was resumed in mid-1943, it was a much more powerful Pacific Fleet that sallied forth.

Action picked up again in June 1943 in both the Atlantic and Pacific. South Dakota, now repaired, was joined by the recently completed Alabama at Scapa Flow, where they stood in for the RN battleships Howe and King George V, freeing the latter from Home Fleet duties for the upcoming HUSKY landings on Sicily. Along with the remaining British battleships Anson, Duke of York and Malaya, and escorted by cruisers Augusta and Tuscaloosa, the two American battleships participated in a demonstration off the coast of Norway hoping to distract attention away from the Mediterranean. Unfortunately German reconnaissance never spotted the allied fleet, ruining the planned deception. Soon thereafter South Dakota departed British waters for the Pacific, where Washington, North Carolina and Indiana had been formed into TF36.3 in support of Operation Cartwheel, the 30 June landings on New Georgia. As would be typical of nearly all such operations for the rest of the war, the three fast battleships were assigned to escort aircraft carriers (in this instance Saratoga and HMS Victorious) while old battleships covered the actual landings with fire support. Indiana was later detached to escort the first of the fast carrier raids, the 31 August strikes on Makin, as part of TF15 composed of Yorktown, Essex and Independence.

The other major occupation of the fast battleships was shore bombardment, as exemplified here by New Jersey off Tinian, 13 June 1944. It is this ability to deliver massive firepower in a hostile environment with great speed and accuracy that has led to the resurrection of New Jersey and her sisters in the 1980s. (USN/NARS)

The two men who directly controlled the movements of the fast battleships during the Battle of Leyte Gulf, when they lost their last chance to engage their Japanese counterparts. (Above) Adm William F. 'Bill' Halsey commanded Third Fleet from New Jersey and was in overall tactical command of operations. Ultimately it was his decision that sent the battleline chasing off after Ozawa's carriers with TF38. (USN/NARS) (Below) VAdm Willis A. 'Ching' Lee (in South Dakota) commanded the fast battleships from their first actions off Guadalcanal through June 1945. He tried to convince Halsey to leave his TF34 behind at San Bernadino Strait but failed. By the time Halsey relented, around noon, it was too late to catch the retreating Kurita. (USN/NARS)

The only real threat to the fast battleships came from the sky. Kamikaze attacks were launched repeatedly against the battleships but few hit and none caused major damage. Smoke billows from Missouri after being hit by a diving Zeke on 11 April 1945 off Okinawa. Damage was minimal, however, and Missouri remained in formation. (USN/NARS)

A victim's view of the same attack. The Zeke hit Missouri's side below main deck level, burning fuel and fragments covered her starboard side amidships. Note the numbering of the 40mm mounts and their associated Mk51 directors. (USN/NHC)

Indiana was back in the Gilberts again on 19 November 1943 as part of TF50.2 along with North Carolina. They were escorting Enterprise, Belleau Wood and Monterey covering OPERATION GALVALNIC landings on Makin. Washington, South Dakota and Massachusetts were assigned to TF50.1 escorting Yorktown, Lexington and Cowpens covering the Mili landings. In part because of the carrier raids of late August, the Gilberts were no longer weakly held by the Japanese who now fought desperately on Makin and particularly Tarawa. The same five fast battleships were employed again on 8 December during carrier raids on Kwajelein. This time all five were joined into a single unit, TF50.8, under the command of RAdm Lee. They approached Nauru under the cover of aircraft from Bunker Hill and Monterey, lobbing 810 16in and 3400 5in shells at the small Japanese garrison. One escorting destroyer was damaged by return fire.

Fast battleships were in action again on 29 January 1944 for OPERATION FLINTLOCK, the Marshalls invasions. They were now eight strong with the addition of Alabama (finally released from Atlantic Fleet duties) and the first two Iowas (Iowa and New Jersey). Again the battleships were split up between carrier groups. Washington, Indiana and Massachusetts were assigned to TG58.1 (Enterprise, Yorktown and Belleau Wood) off Roi and Namur (Kwajelein). North Carolina, South Dakota and Alabama were escorting TG58.2 (Essex, Intrepid and Cabot) off Maloelap. The new Iowa and New Jersey were assigned to TG58.3 (Bunker Hill, Monterey and Cowpens) at Eniwetok. In the early hours of 1 February, during continuing operations off Kwajelein, Indiana and Washington collided, and while neither was seriously damaged, both would be lost to the fleet for several months.

The six remaining fast battleships were recruited for the HAILSTONE raids on Truk, 17-18 February 1944. Iowa and New Jersey were attached to TG50.9, which served as a command unit with Adm Spruance on New Jersey. The other four fast battleships were playing their accustomed role of carrier escort, assigned to TG58.3. A month later, on 18 March, Iowa and New Jersey, again under RAdm Lee and escorted by Lexington and seven destroyers, were formed into TG50.10 for the purpose of bombarding Mille atoll, south of Majuro. During that action, Iowa was hit several times by 15.2cm (6in) shells from the island but suffered no serious damage and never left her place in line. A similar force was organized on 1 May, again under Lee (now a Vice Admiral), for the purpose of raiding Ponape in the Carolines. Seven fast battleships (Indiana having returned) and 10 destroyers with air support from TG58.1 carried out the bombardment without incident.

Again seven fast battleships were joined together for the next operation, though this time it included Washington (with a new bow) in the place of Massachusetts (which was refitting). Formed into TG58.7 (Battle Line), they were intended as a bombardment and battle force in support of OPERATION FORAGER, the Marianas landings. Anticipating a response by the Japanese fleet, Spruance's plans called for Lee's battleships to engage enemy surface forces if the Japanese advanced and to give chase when they retired. The expected battle developed on 19 June 1944, the Battle of the Philippine Sea, popularly known as the Great Marianas Turkey Shoot. As planned, Lee's battleships formed the van unit of the Fifth Fleet. They came under sporadic attack throughout the day from Japanese aircraft heading for the American carriers. During the course of the day South Dakota was hit once and Indiana near-missed.

Spruance's strategy during this three day battle has been criticized by some for a lack of aggressiveness. In particular questions were raised about his decision to turn away from Ozawa late on the 18th, leaving the initiative to the enemy. He was greatly influenced in this decision by Lee, who was reluctant to engage the then undamaged enemy fleet in a night engagement, which was seen as a distinct possibility if Fifth Fleet's westward course was maintained. Lee's caution, curious considering his great desire to finally wield his full battleline in combat, was based on the fear that his battleships, which had rarely had an opportunity to practice as a unit, might do more damage to themselves than to the enemy. Some of his subordinates argued that the risk was worth taking.

While not seriously damaged in this battle, South Dakota was nevertheless sent back to Pearl Harbor for repair. At the same time, North Carolina returned to the west coast for a much needed refit. Thus it was a force of six fast battleships that was available to ADM Halsey's TF38 for the raids on Japanese positions surrounding the Philippine Sea in September and October 1944.

Again the fast battleship force was split up. Iowa and New Jersey (Halsey's flagship) were assigned to TG38.2 and the other four (Washington, Indiana, Massachusetts and Alabama) to TG38.3, with Washington acting as Lee's flagship. These forces supported raids on Palau (6-8 Sept), Mindinao (10 Sept), the Visayas (12-14 Sept) and Luzon (21-22 Sept). During a brief lull following the Luzon raids, South Dakota replaced Indiana which withdrew for refit. The attacks then resumed with raids on Okinawa (10 Oct), Luzon again (11 Oct), Formosa (12-14 Oct) and Luzon yet again (15 Oct). For the subsequent Leyte Gulf landings, beginning on 17 October, Washington and Alabama were transferred from TG38.3 to TG38.4.

The Imperial Japanese Navy responded to the invasion of the Philippines with a final desperate deployment of all available forces, in the process giving Lee his last and best opportunity to again meet major enemy warships in surface battle. Lee's luck failed miserably this time. Not once but twice he would be frustrated.

The fast battleships were still spread out in pairs among Halsey's carrier groups off San Bernardino Strait for most of the day on 24 October. Several airstrikes were launched against the largest of the approaching enemy units, Kurita's Center Force. These attacks succeeded in sinking the super-battleship Musashi and left Kurita in apparent disarray and retreat. At this point, near dusk on 24 October, Ozawa's Northern Force of carriers, intended soley as a diversion, was sighted north of Luzon. Halsey took the bait and at 1512 ordered a run to the north to be led by a Lee's fast battleship, hastily pulled from the carrier groups and formed into TF34.

Lee's protests against withdrawing his battleline from in front of San Bernardino Strait were immediate. He twice tried to no avail to convince Halsey to leave at least part of his force behind, but Halsey was adamant. No forces, not even a picket destroyer, were to remain at San Bernardino.

In slow and dangerous night maneuvers, Lee had to extricate his dispersed forces from their screening positions and concentrate them ahead of the carriers, a process that took most of the night. At dawn on 25 October, TF34 had formed up and was leading Halsey's fleet in a high speed pursuit of Ozawa's carriers just over the horizon to the north. At the same moment Kurita's weakened Center Force was descending on the escort carriers of Taffy 3 off Samar, having debouched unseen from San Bernardino Strait just three hours after Halsey departed. As Halsey was launching his first strikes at Ozawa, Adm Kincaid in Leyte Gulf almost 300 nautical miles to the south was radioing a desperate plea for any and all help. Adm Nimitz back at Pearl Harbor had heard Lee's pleas to Halsey but not the latter's negative reply and was now at a loss to understand how Kurita's force had been able to reach Taffy 3 undetected and why Lee's battleships hadn't intervened. At 1000 he radioed Halsey:

FROM CINCPAC ACTION COM THIRD FLEET INFO COMINCH CTF77 X
WHERE IS RPT WHERE IS TF34 RR THE WORLD WONDERS

The last three words were padding added at Pearl Harbor to throw off enemy decryption but were mistakenly left on the message shown to Halsey that morning. He was furious, thinking that Nimitz was sarcastically criticizing him in front of Adms King (COMINCH) and Kincaid (CTF77). He brooded over the supposed insult for almost an hour before ordering Lee south at high speed at 1055. TF34 arrived off San Bernardino Strait at 0100 on 26 October, Kurita having slipped through three hours before. The final irony was that Lee's battleships had been only 42nm from Ozawa's carriers when it had been ordered south. On both ends of that long futile chase, the fast battleships just missed major action. The battle that would have resulted had even four battleship been left off the exit from San Bernardino Strait would have been cataclysmic. The tactical situation would have been similar to that faced by Oldendorf at Surigao Strait that same night. Lee wouldn't have had Oldendorf's well prepared defense in depth nor his overwhelming superiority in available guns, but Lee would still have been able to 'cap the T' on Kurita's line, concentrating his gunfire on each enemy ship in turn as it emerged from the strait and he would have had the tremendous advantage of radar-directed gunfire. But it wasn't in the cards.

With the failure of this last chance for independent surface action, the fast battleships spent the rest of the war involved in escort duties with occasional shore bombardment to

On 14 July 1945 fast battleships shelled targets on the Japanese mainland for the first time. (Above) The Kamaishi steel works came under fire from the guns of TG 34.8 (South Dakota, Indiana and Massachusetts) under RAdm John Shafroth who replaced Lee in the last months of the war. (USN/NARS) (Below) The steel works, which lay at the head of a small bay, soon was completely obscured by smoke. As the bombardment continued, the battleships secondary batteries engaged a Japanese patrol boat (barely visible against the smoke) that was attempting to cover the escape of three merchantmen caught in the harbor. For the better part of half an hour the little gunboat steamed back and forth across the entrance to the bay, firing away with its little deck gun which couldn't reach halfway to the American battleships, until its charges rounded a headland and made good their escape. (USN/NARS)

relieve the boredom. The only significant detached operation for the remainder of the war came in January 1945 when New Jersey and the recently arrived Wisconsin were dispatched toward Cam Ranh Bay with a cruiser and destroyer escort to ferret out some of Kurita's few remaining big ships reported to be hiding there. The raid was cancelled when further air reconnaissance on 12 January showed the bay empty.

Except for this last incident, the fast battleships' movements were tied to those of the carriers. They escorted repeated raids on Luzon, Okinawa, Indo-China, mainland China, Formosa and finally the 'home islands' of Japan between November 1944 and March 1945. Indiana shelled Iwo Jima singly on 25 January, expending 203 16in shells. During April 1945, the action was largely concentrated around Okinawa with occasional bombardments of enemy strong points. When the carriers returned to Japan in July, the fast battleships went along. South Dakota, Indiana and Massachusetts shelled the Kamaishi steel works on 14 July, the aircraft factory at Hamamatsu on 29-30 July and Kamaishi again on 9 August 1945.

At war's end seven fast battleships assembled in Tokyo Bay though, significantly, they were spread out among four different carrier TGs. The fact that South Dakota served as Nimitz' flagship or that the actual surrender ceremonies ending the war took place on Missouri could do little to obscure the fact that except for one brief flurry of activity early in the war, the fast battleships had spent the war as little more than heavily armored AA platforms.

The end of WWII brought a major debate in a suddenly budget-conscious Navy as to the future role, if any, for the now ten magnificent fast battleships. They represented the ultimate in gun-armed ship development, but were they now iron dinosaurs with no future as the proponents of aircraft so loudly proclaimed? Missouri undertook a highly successful 'Goodwill' cruise in the Mediterranean in 1946 that is credited with helping to stop

Communist expansion in Greece and Turkey. Still, the big ships were expensive to man and maintain and, with no clear mission, it was inevitable that they would be phased out of the active fleet. On 11 September 1946, hardly a year after VJ Day, Indiana was decommissioned. The North Carolinas and the other three South Dakotas followed in 1947. Even the new Iowa began to be 'mothballed' in 1948. New Jersey and Wisconsin were decommissioned that year and Iowa in 1949.

Thus it was only Missouri that remained in active service when the Korean War broke out in 1950. Arriving off Korea in mid-September of that year, she immediately began to use her big guns to great effect. So useful did Missouri prove that the other three Iowas were hastily recommissioned during the course of 1951.

This second tour of duty for the Iowas was actually longer than the first. Through all of 1952, and up until the armistice, the four fast battleships used their big guns in support of land forces off both coasts of Korea. For another two years after the war, all four Iowas remained in commission until the budget-cutters again had their way. Missouri was decommissioned for the first time on 26 February 1955. Her sisters followed during the next two years. When Wisconsin was mothballed on 8 March 1958, the US Navy was without an active battleship for the first time since 1895.

One by one the idle battleships were struck from the Navy List and scrapped. In the early 1950s, a commission had studied the idea of increasing the speed of the six older fast battleships to 31 knots and using them again as fast carrier escorts. However, the cost was considered to be prohibitive and the idea was dropped. North Carolina and Washington were struck on 1 June 1960 (North Carolina being preserved as a memorial). Two years later it was the turn of the four South Dakotas. Two of them, Massachusetts and Alabama, were similarly preserved. If the Vietnam War hadn't intervened, the same fate would probably overtaken the Iowas. The demands of that war, however, led to the reactivation and modernization of New Jersey, which was recommissioned on 8 April 1968. This deployment was short, despite the very positive response of the shore units she supported. Worried diplomats claimed she was too effective '...a destabilizing influence...' inviting enemy superpower response. On 17 December 1969, New Jersey was again placed in reserve.

Again the future looked bleak, as the Iowas languished in mothballs throughout the 1970s. Critics inside the Pentagon wondered why these relics were being preserved. But toward the end of the decade, a few perceptive defense analysts, mostly outside the Pentagon, began to draw some disturbing conclusions about recent naval policy. Since the mid-1960s, the US Navy has been slowly replacing its aging, WWII-vintage surface combatants with newer, 'modern' warships designed for an ocean dominated by carriers and submarines. In common with the ships being built by most other navies (but, significantly, not the Soviet Navy) over the last 20 years, these ships have tended to be small (a destroyer being perceived as a major unit), lightly armed with little besides missiles, with AAW (Anti-Air Warfare) or ASW (Anti-Submarine Warfare) being their primary mission. In most cases, little or no armor was included in the design. In all too many instances, to provide stability on an unarmored hull, superstructures were made of aluminum. Gun armament gradually was downgraded until a 5in gun became the largest piece of artillery in the fleet. Surface combatants existed solely to protect the carriers or hunt an enemy's subs. Should it become necessary to project power ashore, carrier-based tactical airpower (TacAir) could handle the job.

By the end of the 1970s, however, a few critics began to point out flaws in this picture. If the experience in Vietnam wasn't sufficient to point out the fact that air defenses were evolving at least as fast as aircraft, the Israeli experience during the Yom Kippur War was. TacAir could get through, but often at a terrible cost in men and machines. Even if losses in tactical aircraft could be kept down to one percent per strike (a very optimistic figure), the cost in dollars alone of lost aircraft would make the employment of TacAir in a long-term operation such as beachhead support nearly prohibitive. And even if this cost is considered acceptable, the problem remains that a pair of carriers (the standard tactical unit) couldn't supply the continual fire support that would be required by a landing force on a hostile shore. Nor could the problem be solved to any great extent by available ship-mounted guns. A 5in gun lacks sufficient range or weight of shell to be effective much

Gradually the fast battleships were paid off after WWII, with the exception of Missouri which remained in commission and was available at the outbreak of the Korean War. Because there was little air threat to the carriers and no surface opposition to worry about, the other three Iowas were reactivated and used extensively along with Missouri for shore bombardment. Here Iowa shells Kojo during joint amphibious exercises, 15 October 1952. (USN)

Eventually, the budget-cutters caught up with the Iowas again and they were again mothballed. Wisconsin, New Jersey and Iowa (left to right) lie moored side-by-side at Philadelphia, April 1967. (USN)

past the shoreline. And the question remains whether these small ships could survive shore-based retaliation. Aluminum burns, as the US Navy forcibly found out with the near loss of the cruiser Belknap in 1975 after collision with the carrier Kennedy. The experience of the Royal Navy off the Falklands, in which four major combatants (destroyers and frigates) were lost and others put out of action by damage that probably wouldn't have been life-threatening to an equivalent WWII-era ship, must be heeded.

The alternative to expensive and possibly ineffective TacAir and inadequate, vulnerable gun platforms is the same option that was available in 1944, the fast battleship. The calls for the re-activation of the Iowas began to be heard increasingly toward the end of the 1970s.* The logic is impeccable. A pair of aircraft carriers can deliver about 420 tons of ordnance ashore in twelve hours of operation. A battleship firing nine 16in guns can deliver the same weight in 18 minutes. While TacAir has a range of several hundred miles compared to only about 20nm (firing conventional projectiles) for a battleship, this may be more than adequate. It has been estimated that 80% of TacAir targets hit during the Vietnam War would have been within the range of a battleship's guns. In terms of accuracy of delivery, the advantage is very much with the battleship. In comparison with the 5''/54cal gun now employed on most US Navy ships, the 16'/50cal gun of the Iowa class is vastly superior in every category except rate of fire. A 5in shell weighs approximately 70lb, has a range of about 13nm and can penetrate about 6ft of concrete. A 16in shell weighs between 1900 and 2700lb, has a range of over 20nm and can penetrate 30ft of concrete. With new technologies the capability of the 16in shell could be boosted even further. A sub-caliber, laser-guided shell has been proposed that might have a range of almost 50nm. With 12in side armor and all-steel construction, the Iowas would be relatively immune to the Exocets or 500lb bombs that devastated the British fleet off the Falklands.

Despite mounting arguments in favor of reactivating the Iowas, as long as naval

budgets were as restricted as they were during Carter's presidency, there was little likelihood of it ever coming to pass. The election of Ronald Reagan in 1980 and his subsequent promise to rebuild the Navy to a 600-ship force level provided the needed impetus. Reagan's FY81 defense budget included money for the reactivation of New Jersey. FY82 likewise included monies for Iowa and plans were made for subsequent budgets to provide for the similar reactivation of Missouri and Wisconsin. Not surprisingly, given recent political history, this funding process hasn't gone quite as planned. New Jersey has been refitted and modernized and was recommissioned in an impressive ceremony at Long Beach Naval Shipyard on 28 December 1982. Iowa's more extensive modernization was fully funded and her recommissioning took place on 28 April 1984. Funds for the other two Iowas have yet to be approved by Congress. Perhaps the strong impression made by New Jersey's appearances off Nicaragua and Lebanon in her first year of reactivation will convince the reluctant.

New Jersey has been deployed as the nucleus of an independent surface action group capable of sustained attack on hostile shore installations or ships. It has taken 40 years, but it now appears that a role has been found for the remaining fast battleships that exploits the strengths of their design. At last, it appears that the fast battleships will be employed in the role for which they were originally conceived, the projection of decisive force wherever it may be needed.

*Most of the arguments in this section are taken from 'A Sea-Based Interdiction System for Power Projection' by Charles E. Myers, Jr., published in the November 1979 issue of US Naval Institute Proceedings. Mr. Myers was one of the chief proponents of battleship reactivation throughout this period.

North Carolina Class
BB55 North Carolina
BB56 Washington

The complex process that led to the final configuration of this the first class of battleships for the US Navy since 1923 resulted in a highly successful design. The greatest problem for the designers was providing an adequate measure of armor, armament and speed within the constraints of the 35,000 ton treaty limit. This amounted to an increase of less than 2500 tons over the preceding Colorado class (as built). Yet on a tonnage increase of less than ten per cent, the new battleships were to be significantly more capable. One more 16in gun was to be carried (9 vs. 8), seven more knots of speed to be achieved (28 vs. 21) and similar armor protection was to be carried on a significantly longer hull (728 vs. 624ft).

This improvement was achieved only through considerable design innovation. For instance, the armor belt of the North Carolinas was exactly four inches thinner than the earlier Colorados', but being inclined at 15 degrees it offered similar protection while saving vital weight that was used to improve horizontal protection and provide a torpedo bulge. This level of protection was considered adequate against a 14in battery, such as the North Carolinas were originally intended to mount. A basic rule of thumb of warship design is that a ship's armor should be able to resist the equivalent of its own gunfire. Against 14in fire, the North Carolinas' protection gave an adequate immune zone (19,000-30,000yd). Against 16in guns firing the then standard 2240lb shell, the immune zone was much smaller (21,300-27,800yd). Similar weight savings were achieved by using triple mounts for the 16in guns in the place of the Colorados' twin mounts, reducing the number of turrets and barbettes by one while increasing the number of guns. Finally, the use of compact high-pressure, high-temperature boilers and reliable high-speed, double reduction turbines not available when the Colorados were built allowed savings in weight and size of the powerplant while increasing power more than four times (121,000shp vs. 27,200shp). Despite all of these exertions, the North Carolinas came in somewhat over the treaty restrictions. Both had a standard displacement of 36,600 tons.

The efficacy of the North Carolinas' defensive scheme was displayed when the North

North Carolina, nearing completion at the New York Navy Yard early in 1941. Main and secondary armament have been fitted but none of the lighter AA is in place and her Mk 38 main armament directors are still missing. Note the scaffolding around her tower mast. (USN/NHC)

North Carolina at her commissioning on 9 April 1941 at New York, still far from complete. She is painted in the prewar measure, overall Navy Gray. (USN/NHC)

North Carolina 1942

Washington 1944

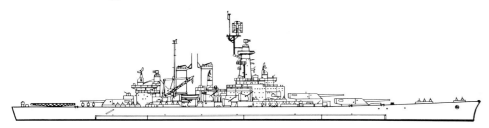

Carolina was torpedoed on 15 September 1942. The torpedo hit on the portside below No.1 turret, blowing a hole 32x18ft in the shell plating. Three armor plates were cracked, the turret race of Number One turret was damaged (rendering the turret inoperable), shock effects knocked out the SC radar and about 970 tons of sea water were shipped. Despite this damage, with 480 tons of counterflooding North Carolina was able to increase speed to 25 knots and maintain formation in Hornet's screen until dusk.

Two weeks after her commissioning, Washington leaves the Philadelphia Navy Yard for her first shakedown on 29 May 1941. She still lacks all light armament and her big rangefinders. She is painted in the Ms 1 scheme. (USN/NARS)

North Carolina briefly carried the Ms 1 scheme and then was painted into Ms 12 with Ms 5 false bow wave, an unusual combination. She carries her first radar fit, a CXAM-1 air search antenna on her foremast. Note that she now finally has her large Mk 38 main-battery directors in place. (USN/NARS)

(Above) North Carolina on her Hypo Run, April 1942. Her camouflage is the Ms 12 (Modified). When built, North Carolina had a small supplementary low-angle director in front of her forward Mk37, but by this time it has been deleted to make room for additional AA and their local directors. (USN/NARS)

(Left) Washington being inclined at Hvalfjord, Iceland, in June 1942, where she was based when not actually at Scapa Flow. In addition to a CXAM-1 on her foremast, she has FD fire control radars on her Mk 37 directors. She is painted in an Ms 12 (Modified) 'Splotch' scheme. (USN/NARS)

(Below) When she went to war in June of 1942, North Carolina carried FC main battery fire control radars on her Mk 38 directors. (USN/NARS via Dave Shadell)

Seen from one of Wasp's aircraft at the time of the Battle of the Eastern Solomons, North Carolina displays a unique variation on the Ms 12 Mod standard. All horizontal surfaces were supposed to have been painted Deck Blue, but North Carolina had wavy bands of a lighter color (possibly Haze Gray) painted along her deck edge to create the illusion of a smaller ship, 24 August 1942. (USN/NARS)

Now painted in Ms 21, North Carolina is seen on 5 August 1943 after her repair and refit at Pearl Harbor. Her radar suite is the same as before except she now carries an SG surface search antenna on her mainmast. Her AA fit has been considerably strengthened with fourteen additional quad 40mm mounts and numerous single 20s. (NASM)

The North Carolina class remained essentially as built for the entire war, except for continual upgrades to the electronics suite and AA defenses. The heavy anti-aircraft batteries were 20x5in/38cal DPs in twin turrets which remained unaltered during their career. The development of the VT proximity fuse for the 5in shell made this gun a very effective defense against the Kamikaze late in the war. In contrast, the medium and light AA batteries went through continual revision. Both ships were completed with 16x1.1in quads and 12x.50cal in single mounts. The former proved unreliable and the latter too light to be effective and both were soon replaced. Fortunately these problems had been anticipated and during the course of 1941 BuOrd had been testing all available designs in search of adequate replacements. Production licenses were obtained for the Swiss 20mm Oerlikon to meet light AA needs (.50cal is 12.7mm) and for the Swedish 40mm Bofors for the medium. By war's end, North Carolina carried 15x40mm quads and 36x20mm. Washington carried the same number of Bofors and no less than 83 singly-mounted Oerlikons.

Washington collided with Indiana during maneuvers off Kwajelein in the early morning of 1 February 1944. Both ships were in darkened condition when Indiana turned out of formation to refuel destroyers. In doing so she pulled across Washington's path. In the resulting collision Washington's bow was demolished back to Frame 21 but flooding was minor. Repairs were completed and she was back in service by 30 May. (USN/NHC)

(Above and Below) Starboard and port views of Washington as she completed repairs at Puget Sound, 26 April 1944. She is painted in Ms 22. The regulation called for the border between the Navy Blue and the Haze Gray to parallel the waterline at the height of the lowest point of main deck sheer. In this case neither the letter nor the spirit of the regulation has been followed. Her AA fit resembles North Carolina's except that she has one additional Bofors mount, located on her aft 16in turret. She has SG radars on both masts, an SK air search antenna forward and FH fire control radars on her Mk 38 directors. (USN/NARS)

(Above and Below) Toward the end of 1943, North Carolina replaced her Ms 21 camouflage with this striking Ms 32/18D scheme. Her radar suite and AA fit resembled Washington's. For some reason, probably due to signal interference, she and her sister carried the FD radar on their aft Mk 37 director on an extended mount. The above view dates from 12 November 1943; the below from 25 January 1944. (USN/NARS & NASM)

(Above and Below) North Carolina underwent an extended refit in late Summer 1944, emerging with an updated radar suite. The FD radars on her Mk 37 directors have been replaced by the improved Mk 12/22 and the SK air search antenna on her foremast has been replaced by an SK-2. Her camouflage has been repainted with minor variations. (USN/NARS)

Sometime in early 1945 North Carolina was repainted in Ms 22, which she wore for the rest of her active life. These sailors touch up the countershading on a 16in gun barrel during operations off Japan, July 1945. (USN/NARS)

North Carolina remained in service for less than two years after the war ended. She was overhauled one last time early in 1946 at New York and emerged minus one pair of Bofors mounts and nearly all of her light AA, 3 June 1946. (USN via Jim Sullivan)

Washington is about to join up with the fleet oiler Naskaskia (AO-27) off Okinawa, 5 April 1945. She ended the war with essentially the same equipment fit she carried the year before. (USN/NARS)

South Dakota Class

BB57 South Dakota
BB58 Indiana
BB59 Massachusetts
BB60 Alabama

The design of the South Dakota class was influenced by the same constraints as the North Carolinas because they too were intended to meet the Washington Treaty limits. The difference was that they were designed from the outset to carry a 16in main battery. In keeping with the 'rule of thumb' about warship armor, this required a twenty-five per cent improvement in protection over the North Carolinas. On a fixed displacement, however, an increase in one feature always forces sacrifices somewhere else. Again, innovative design solved most of the problems. By inclining the armor another four degrees (to nineteen degrees), adding another 1/4in (to a maximum of 12 1/4in) and mounting the armor belt in from the ship's side plating, it was possible to create an excellent immune zone of 17,700-30,900yd against the then standard 2240lb 16in shell. However, advances in ordnance technology obsoleted the standard shell and when completed, the South Dakotas (and North Carolinas) actually fired a heavier (2700lb) armor piercing shell at reduced muzzle velocity, sacrificing some range to gain increased penetration. Against this shell, the South Dakotas' immune zone shrank to a barely adequate 20,500-26,400yd.

The entire space between the internal armor belt, which tapered all the way down to the ship's bottom, and the outer hull formed an extended torpedo cavity divided by three longitudinal bulkheads. In theory this system should have provided better protection than the North Carolinas' external torpedo bulges. Fortunately they were never tested in combat. However when Indiana was rammed by Washington in the starboard quarter forward of number three turret, she took on much more water than anticipated. An inquiry concluded that had the damage extended much further aft, Indiana might have been in danger of sinking.

This armor scheme provided almost double the protection against heavy fire in comparison to the North Carolinas, but at a cost. It was almost a half ton heavier per foot of armor belt. The only way that this extra weight could fit into a 35,000 ton ship would be by shortening the length of the armored citadel. Waterline length of the South Dakotas was therefore reduced by 48.5ft (to 666ft) and the distance between the fore and aft armored bulkheads decreased by 75ft (to 375ft). In the give and take of ship design, this reduction in length without a simultaneous reduction in beam (not possible because of the volume required for the powerplant) meant that the South Dakotas had a much fuller hull form and consequently required 11.5 per cent more power (135,000 vs 121,000shp) to achieve the same top speed. Only by ingenious use of space and advanced technology was BuShips able to provide this increased power in machinery space reduced in length by almost 25 per cent.

The fuller hull form and vertical sides of the South Dakotas made them both more maneuverable and more stable than the North Carolinas. Their increased protection made them better fighting ships in every combat category. Only in the area of habitability did the earlier class have an advantage. Crew spaces on the South Dakotas were far more cramped but still exceeded by a comfortable margin those of any other navy.

The protective system of the South Dakotas had only one real combat test. In the Second Naval Battle of Guadalcanal, South Dakota was hit by twenty-seven shells ranging in caliber from 5in to 14in. While damage to unprotected areas was extensive and fires in the superstructure and damage to radars forced South Dakota out of the action, she suffered no serious flooding and never was her basic combat capability seriously impaired. The loss of her radars in night combat, however, was a psychological blow of major proportion. In the short time that radar had been in the fleet, ships had become totally dependent on their aid for night action. The loss of her radar left South Dakota feeling blindfolded and at a disadvantage compared to the radar-less enemy. This feeling of dependence and

Her guns quiet but still maneuvering at high speed, South Dakota at Santa Cruz during a lull in the action, 26 October 1942, as seen from Portland. She is painted in the Ms 21 navy blue she wore for the rest of the war. She carries her original radar suite, FC radars on her Mk 38 main battery directors, FD radars on her Mk 37 high-angle directors, an SG sea search set on the front of her tower mast and an SC air search antenna on her foremast. (NASM)

Indiana 1942

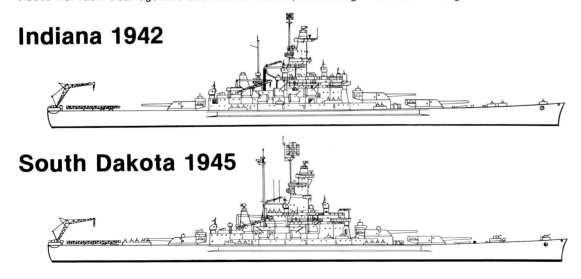

South Dakota 1945

Indiana at Newport News in August of 1942 prior to sailing for the Pacific is painted in what is believed to be the little-known Ms 15 disruptive scheme. Claims have been made that the colors are three shades of green and there are reports of an unidentified green battleship being seen in the South Pacific in late 1942, but there are a number of reasons to doubt this. It is much more likely that the colors here are standard navy Purple-Blues (Navy Blue, Ocean Gray and Haze Gray). Lacking hard evidence this debate can't be resolved, but what is known for sure is that Indiana did not carry this scheme into combat. By the time she reported to Noumea for combat duty she was painted in Ms 22. Indiana's radars are similar to South Dakota's except that FH fire control radar is being fitted to her main battery rangefinders. (USN/NARS)

radar's proven vulnerability in combat were the primary motivation behind the rapid proliferation and often redundant radar systems on major ships.

Only South Dakota, the first of the class to be commissioned, ever carried 1.1in and .50cal AA mounts. South Dakota also differed from the rest of the class in carrying two fewer 5in twin turrets. Intended as a flagship, South Dakota sacrificed these turrets to allow a larger conning tower to be added. Her initial medium and light AA fit was 7x1.1in quads, 16x20mm and 8x.50cal. By war's end, this had increased to 17x40mm quads and 77x20mm. Indiana was built with 7x40mm quads and 16x20mm and ended the war with 14x40mm quads and 52x20mm. Massachusetts was completed with the same number of 40mm quad mounts and 35x20mm and finished with 18x40mm and 33x20mm. Alabama also was built with 7x40mm quads as well as 22x20mm and ended the war with 14x40mm quads and 56x20mm.

The colors worn by Alabama during her working up are known from contemporary color photos showing her in Navy Blue, Ocean Gray and Haze Gray. The question remains whether this was the largely experimental Ms 15 or just a degenerate Ms 12. Her radar suite resembles that of her two older sisters. Light and medium AA is proliferating in every open deck space. Note the empty tubs aft for two more quad 40s, indicative of the fact that at this stage of the war demand exceeded supply, 1 December 1942. (USN/NARS)

Indiana seen from Saratoga soon after arrival at Noumea, 17 December 1942, repainted in Ms 22 for her first tour of combat. Both ships were supporting the continuing action on Guadalcanal. The only other battleships to serve in the South Pacific during this period (North Carolina, Washington and South Dakota) wore Ms 12 or Ms 21, making it likely that the reported Green battleship never actually existed. (USN/NARS)

Alabama similarly painted out its disruptive camouflage scheme with an Ms 22 scheme before arriving in the Pacific at the end of June 1943. Her radar suite is unchanged, but the AA fit has been upgraded. In particular, quad 40mm mounts have replaced multiple 20s atop Turrets No.2 and No.3, 9 August 1943. (USN/NARS)

Massachusetts was painted in Ms 22 for her Torch activities and stayed in that scheme for the rest of the war. Like Alabama, she arrived in the Pacific in mid-1943 in time for the beginning of the Central Pacific campaign. (USN/NARS)
evidence. (USN/NARS)

Alabama, **December 1942 in the Atlantic carrying the splotched Measure 15 scheme.**

Starboard side of Indiana **in January of 1944 at Majuro painted in the disruptive Measure 32 scheme.**

Port side of Indiana **at Majuro in the Measure 32 scheme.**

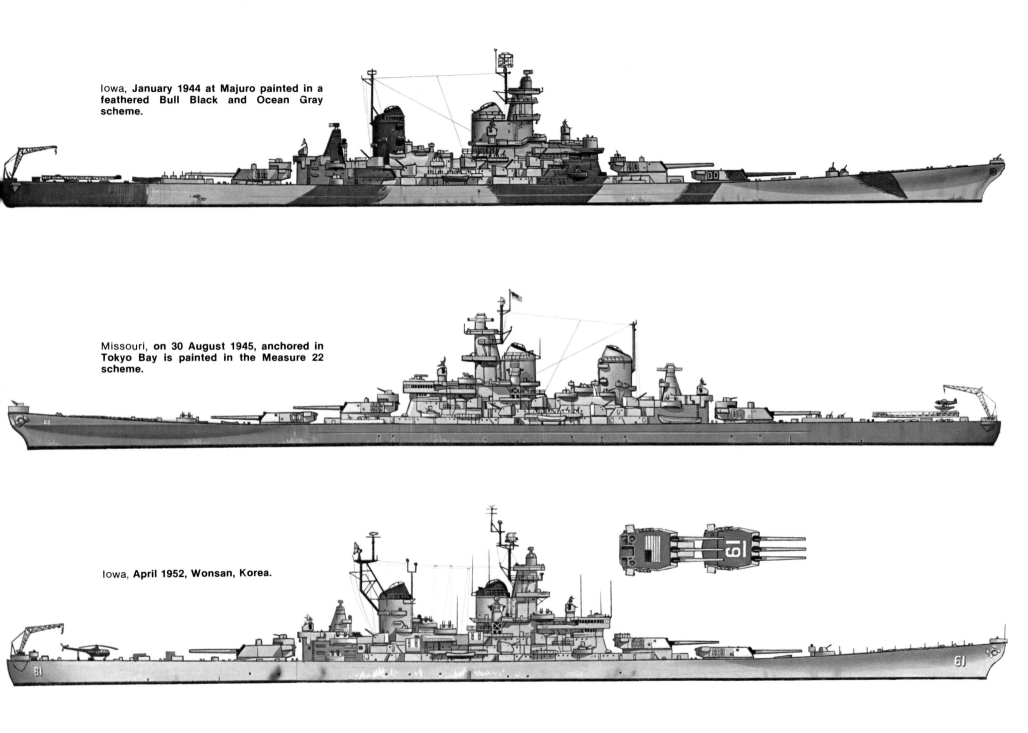

Iowa, **January 1944 at Majuro painted in a feathered Bull Black and Ocean Gray scheme.**

Missouri, **on 30 August 1945, anchored in Tokyo Bay is painted in the Measure 22 scheme.**

Iowa, **April 1952, Wonsan, Korea.**

Alone among the South Dakotas, Indiana adopted an Ms 32 disruptive camouflage scheme during the mid-war period when such schemes became popular. While the Ms 21 scheme was designed to conceal a ship from the air (and succeeded as long as the ship wasn't leaving a wake) and the Ms 22 was an effective anti-submarine measure (the standard Atlantic scheme from mid-1942), the mid-war disruptive schemes (Ms 31, 32 and 33) were general-purpose measures intended primarily to protect against observation by surface opponents. The theory was that at a distance the colors would blur together to make a middle tone that would conceal, while at close range the jagged edges would break up the ship's silhouette and make determination of her course more difficult. The problem was that they were totally ineffective against aerial observation and when the kamikaze threat became serious in late 1944, these schemes tended to disappear in favor of Ms 21. Note how the Ms 32 camouflage is carried over her deck. Indiana's radar suite has been somewhat altered since December 1942. An SK radar has replaced the SC on her foremast and her SG has been moved from the forward face of her tower mast to the top of her mainmast. Her fire control radars remain the same except that an FC antenna has been sited atop her conning tower. All eight fast battleships then in commission were gathered in support of the OPERATION FLINTLOCK, the invasion of the Marshalls (Roi, Maloelap, Kwajelein and Eniwetok). While thus engaged, Indiana and Washington collided during night maneuvers off Kwajelein on 1 February 1944. (USN/NARS)

(Above) South Dakota seen at the time of the Marshalls landings, 25 January 1944. She remained in her early Ms 21 throughout the war. Her radar suite resembles Indiana's, except that she has retained the original SG set on the tower mast as well as having a second antenna installed on her mainmast. This view shows particularly well the differences between South Dakota and her sisters. Fitted as a flagship, her armored conning tower is a deck higher than her sisters'. To compensate for this additional weight, she lacks the middle 5in turret on each broadside carried by the rest of the class. (USN/NARS)

(Below) Emerging from refit at Puget Sound, Massachusetts is seen off Point Wilson, WA, on 11 July 1944. Her radar has been upgraded in similar fashion to Indiana's, except that the FD radar on her Mk37 directors has been replaced by the more advanced Mk12/22 combination. She has the taller mainmast that eventually was fitted to all of her sisters. As with all capital ships refitting at this time, Massachusetts has much enhanced medium AA fit, with no less than 18 quad 40mm mounts. (USN/NARS)

(Above) Alabama, one of the many ships in the Pacific Fleet to revert to the Ms 21 camouflage in 1944, is seen from Essex near Majuro late in the year. Like South Dakota she has retained her forward SG while adding a second on her mainmast. In comparison with Massachusetts she is carrying a much lighter AA fit, with only 12 Bofors mounts in carried there by some escort carriers. This is believed to have been its only use in the Pacific. (USN/NARS)

(Below) Post-collision and repair, Indiana looks much the same as she did before, except that she's traded in her FD radars for Mk122 and her Ms 32 camouflage for a more sedate Ms 22, 6 January 1945. Like Massachusetts, she has the more substantial mainmast, on which she carries an SC-2 air search antenna on a new tilting mount allowing a measure of radar coverage directly over the ship (zenith search). (USN/NARS)

Alabama coming home. It is possible to make out the details of her radar suite which has been much modified since February. On her mainmast is an SK-2 air search set and a pair of TDY jamming radomes, with an SR air search antenna and an SG on her mainmast. The camouflage is Ms 22. (USN/NHC)

With her long 'paying off' pennant trailing back to her aircraft handling crane, South Dakota enters San Francisco Bay in September 1945. She was probably the least modified of her class, her camouflage and radar suite being little changed since early 1944. She now has her name painted across her stern, a sure sign that the war is over. (USN/NHC)

On a high speed run in Puget Sound, Indiana is seen from Breton (CVE-23) in February 1946. Her radar suite and camouflage is identical to Alabama's. She was placed in reserve in September 1946 and decommissioned a year later. Some consideration was given to re-engining the South Dakotas to increase their speed, but it never got beyond the planning stage. (USN/NARS)

Iowa Class

BB61 Iowa
BB62 New Jersey
BB63 Missouri
BB64 Wisconsin
BB65 Illinois (cancelled)
BB66 Kentucky (cancelled)

The Iowas were designed after the restrictions of the naval treaties had finally expired. Freed from the 35,000 ton limit, BuShips finally was able to design the fast battleship it had always wanted. Keeping the main battery and armor scheme of the South Dakotas, the Iowas increased speed by five knots (to 32 1/2 knots). In order to gain this extra speed, power was increased by 77,000shp (to 212,000shp). In order to find room for the increased powerplant necessary to produce this extra speed, the hull of the Iowas were increased to 860ft, 194ft longer than the South Dakotas, and much finer. The most important innovation in this design was the adoption of a new, longer 16in gun. The Iowas mounted

16in/50cal guns which took advantage of the full capabilities of the heavier, 2700lb AP shell. Higher muzzle velocities from a heavier charge gave more than 5000 yards greater range (to 42,345yd - over 21 nautical miles).

All four Iowas were completed with 10x5in DP twin turrets. Iowa, the first to be finished, carried 15x40mm quads and 60x20mm at completion. The other three in the class were completed with 20x40mm quads and 49x20mm. Iowa finished the war with 19x40mm quads and 52x20mm. The other three finished with the same number of Bofors mounts as when built but each had a different number of Oerlikons. New Jersey had 57, Missouri had 43 and Wisconsin had 51.

As the only class of fast battleships to see action after WWII, the Iowas were the only ones modified to counter the changing airborne threat of the post war years. The first change was the removal of almost all 20mm mounts within two years of VJ Day. During the later part of WWII, the Oerlikon was increasingly found to be too light to stop an attacking aircraft. It gained the derisive nickname 'doorknocker' because it did little more than announce the presence of incoming aircraft. At the same time, the number of Bofors

A floating AA battery! Crewmen on Iowa point skyward at a target during gunnery practice in May of 1943. All three calibers of AA (20mm, 40mm and 5in) are visible. The light 20mm Oerlikons were much criticized during the war as being ineffective, particularly against kamikazes which had to be destroyed rather than just damaged. The 40mm Bofors were popular because they trained rapidly and fired a substantial shell of almost two pounds weight, frequently capable of deflecting a diving kamikaze. The 5in/38, particularly after the introduction of the VT (Variable Time) proximity fuze, was an extremely useful DP gun. A measure of each gun's popularity can be seen in the length of its postwar service. The Oerlikons disappeared at the end of WWII; the Bofors remained, in reduced numbers, until after the Korean War; the 5in/38 remains in use today. (USN/NARS)

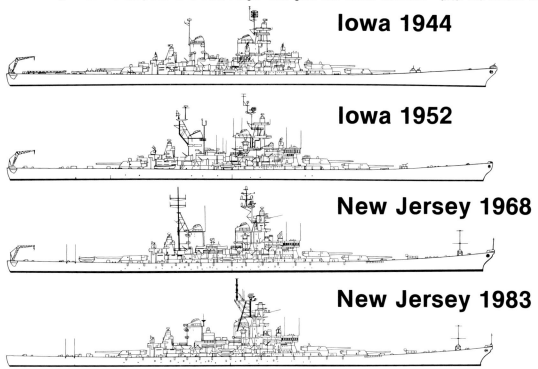

Iowa 1944

Iowa 1952

New Jersey 1968

New Jersey 1983

New Jersey's original radar suite, Philadelphia Navy Yard, 8 July 1943. Antenna designations beginning with 'F' indicated fire control radars, with 'S' indicating search radars and 'B' standing for IFF antennas. (USN/NHC)

quad mounts was reduced to fourteen. This was the medium AA fit of all four Iowas during their Korean War service and the shape in which they were retired in the late 1950s. When New Jersey was reactivated for service off Vietnam, all remaining 40mm mounts were removed. Aircraft had gotten so big and fast that the 40mm now was no longer considered an effective weapon.

Only in the latest incarnation of the Iowas have new weapons been installed. To add to her offensive punch, sixteen Harpoon anti-ship cruise missiles in four quad mounts have been fitted to New Jersey. Four armored box launchers for a total of thirty-two Tomahawk nuclear or conventional warhead cruise missiles have also been added. For defense against incoming anti-ship missiles, four Phalanx multi-barrel 20mm Close-In Weapons System (CIWS) have been mounted. Capable of firing 50rps, the CIWS has integral closed-loop radar which tracks both an incoming target and outgoing rounds for continuous updating. As a further defensive measure, four tubes for SRBOC chaff rockets are fitted on each side. To make room for the new weapons, four of the ten original 5in turrets have been removed. Sensor upgrades include the fitting of an SPS-49 long-range two dimensional air search radar, SLQ-32 passive ESM sensors and WSC-3 satellite navigation equipment. Current plans call for all four Iowas to be reactivated in this configuration. New Jersey completed her sea trials in October 1982 and was recommissioned on 28 December 1982. Iowa was moved to the Litton-Ingalls shipyard at Pascagoula, MS, during 1982 for her modernization. The recommissioning of the remaining Iowas, Congress willing, is scheduled to follow New Jersey at intervals of about 18 months.

A second stage of reconstruction for the Iowas has been mooted, though there will undoubtedly be resistance from Congress. Phase II plans are far from firm but tentatively call for the removal of No.3 turret and its replacement by a vertical launcher for as many as 400 missiles or a hanger and 'ski-jump' for VTOL aircraft or a combination of the two.

Montana Class

While the Iowas were released from the constraints of the 35,000 ton treaty limit, their design wasn't totally free from restrictions. The width of the locks of the Panama Canal restricted beam to 108ft, the same as that of the North Carolinas and South Dakotas. One last class of battleships was designed by the US Navy that disregarded this final limitation. The Montana class would have added a fourth triple 16in turret and 30ft of length to the Iowa design. Even accepting a reduction in power and speed (172,000shp and 28 knots), displacement would have risen to 60,500 tons. Five Montanas were planned and two were actually ordered but all were cancelled in 1943 before any keels were laid.

Later Air Search Radars

SK

SK-2

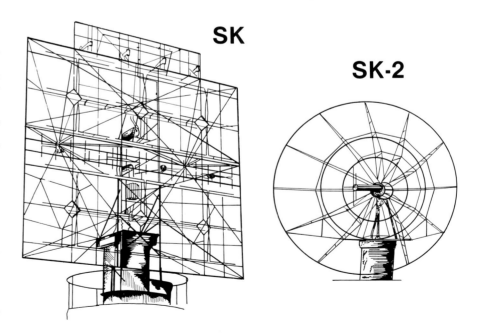

Iowa goes to war, Kwajelein, 24 January 1944. Her radar suite differs from New Jersey's only in that she has an FC antenna on her conning tower. Her camouflage is a very unusual combination of Dull Black and Ocean Gray with one edge of each panel of Black being feathered into the Gray. This scheme was developed for use in the Atlantic and was carried there by some escort carriers. This is believed to have been its only use in the Pacific. (USN/NARS)

The 16in/50 gun in triple turrets was the Iowas' main punch. Each barrel could hurl an armor-piercing shell weighing more than a ton over a range of 21nm. (USN/NARS)

All of that power is of little use if the target can't be sighted and accurately ranged. Each of the Iowas' main battery turrets had an integral rangefinder allowing for local fire control in an emergency. Under normal circumstances, sighting and ranging was to be done by the long-base rangefinders (26.5ft) in the fore and aft Mk 38 directors. With the advent of radar, these tasks were taken over by fire control radars (for ranging) such as the FH and surface search radars (for sighting) such as the SG. All four of these items are visible in this view of Iowa's Turret 3, aft tower and mainmast, May 1943. (USN/NARS)

Fire Control Radars

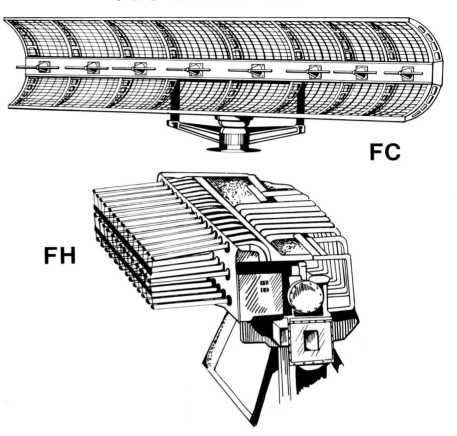

FC

FH

The 16 Inch Gun

The Iowa class battleships mounted nine 16in/50cal Mark 7 guns. Besides the 2700lb AP round, the gun also fired a 1900lb high-capacity projectile with a high explosives charge of 154lb. For shore bombardment there is a reduced charge (315lb of powder vs the 660lb normal charge) to reduce barrel wear. (Large caliber naval guns have a replaceable barrel liner which has a life of about 200 normal rounds before wear to the rifling affects accuracy. Barrel liner replacement is a major operation that can only be done at a shipyard.) For New Jersey's Vietnam deployment, a new cooler burning powder was adopted, also with the aim of prolonging barrel life. With this charge, a 2700lb AP round has a range 40,185yd.

The reborn Iowas will fire the same type of rounds, at least at first. On the drawing boards are sub-caliber rounds that would increase range to approximately 50 nautical miles. Add to this the possibility of terminal guidance and power boost for 'mid-course correction' and the power of this gun may become even more awesome.

16in shells are stored on two levels of the barbette in circular chambers surrounding the rotating turret structure. Because of their great weight, 2700lb for these APC shells, they were moved by means of chains looped around capstans such as that in the foreground. Similar chains hold the shells in position until needed. They are delivered to the turret by three shell hoists (one for each barrel), one of which is in the center of this view. (USN/NARS)

Three crewmen serve the turret rangefinder, in case local control becomes necessary. The seat for the middle crewman is on top of the chain rammer housing of the central barrel, making for a rough ride. (USN/NARS)

At the lowest levels of the barbette are the powder handling rooms. Powder charges in cloth bags, each weighing about 90lb, are passed through scuttles from the magazines and carried to the powder hoists (two — one for the left and center guns and one for the right). Generally, six such charges were needed for each barrel each time the gun was fired. Each turret had a complement of about 75 men, who could fire a salvo every 30 seconds. (USN/NARS)

Just prior to leaving for war, New Jersey lies at Hampton Roads, VA, 7 September 1943. She wears the Ms 21 camouflage she carried for most of the war. In the background is the French battleship Richelieu, sister of the Jean Bart, which had just completed a major refit. Her camouflage is similar to that carried by Iowa. Richelieu would make an interesting comparison with one of the North Carolinas, being roughly contemporary and also designed to stay within treaty limits, but she comes off second bd was Mk 122 radars on her Mk 37 directors. (USN/NARS)

Missouri carried this dramatic Ms 32/22D camouflage while working up in the Atlantic, but painted it out before leaving for the Pacific, 1 August 1944. Her original radar suite differed from her two older sisters in having the newer SK-2 antenna on her foremast and Mk 122 radars on her Mk 37 directors. (USN/NARS)

On her way to war, Missouri carried the more sedate and practical Ms 22 scheme, seen here on 26 December 1944. Though laid down third in her class, Missouri took longer to complete than Wisconsin and was the last of the fast battleships to enter combat. (USN/NARS)

(Above) New Jersey at war, 24 January 1944, differs only in details from her appearance during her working up. One additional pair of quad 40mm mounts are carried just forward of No.3 turret. (USN/NARS)

(Below) Virtually all combat seen by fast battleships was defense against enemy aircraft, particularly kamikazes. Here, Missouri is shrouded in the smoke of her own AA off Okinawa, 11 April 1945. (USN/NARS)

(Below Right) Sometimes even the best defense fails. On that day, Missouri was crashed by a single kamikaze on her starboard side amidships. Kamikazes may have been murder on vulnerable carriers and destroyers but this one barely scratched Missouri, doing little more than start a gasoline fire that was quickly extinguished. She never left her place in formation around Yorktown. (USN/NARS)

(Below) Wisconsin, seen working up in April 1944, is wearing the Ms 22 camouflage in which she was commissioned and in which she fought out WWII. (USN/NARS)

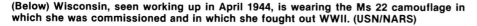

Missouri was chosen as the site of the Japanese surrender in Tokyo Bay (Sagami Wan) on 2 September 1945. Fujiyama rises behind Missouri's bow as she rests at anchor off the Japanese capital, 30 August 1945. Since her combat career in WWII was so short (less than a year), there hasn't been time for any significant changes to be made to her external appearance. Her radar and AA fits look much as they did a year earlier. (USN/NARS)

(Right) The actual surrender took place next to No.2 turret on Missouri's starboard side. The Allied commanders, Gen MacArthur and Adm Nimitz, stride up to the microphones, followed by Adm Halsey. (USN/NHC)

The closest New Jersey ever got to a Japanese battleship was in Tokyo Bay where she anchored only a few hundred yards from the now impotent Nagato, 30 December 1945. New Jersey now wears the almost standard Ms 22 camouflage. Her radar suite has been totally revamped since her entry into the war. She now has an Mk 13 fire control radar on her forward Mk 38 main battery director while retaining the older FH on her aft Mk 38. She carries an SK-2 air search antenna, an SG sea search antenna and an SCR-720 night-fighter control radome on her foremast and an SP height finder and another SG on her mainmast. (USN/NARS)

Missouri and her three sisters were used extensively for shore bombardment during the Korean War. Here she lobs a salvo from No.2 turret at Chong Jin, near the Chinese border, 21 October 1950. Note the almost complete disappearance of 20mm Oerlikon light AA guns (a pair still remain at the bow). Her radar suite looks similar to that seen on New Jersey in 1945 except that her SK-2 has been replaced by what appears to be an SR-3 long range air search set. (USN)

Korea

Since there was virtually no threat in the air or on the sea against which the Iowas had to be concealed, no attempt was made to camouflage them. They remained in the standard peacetime overall navy gray. In fact, the only possible airborne threat came from friendly aircraft. Therefore Missouri and all her sisters carried their hull numbers and a large national flag painted on the roof of No.1 turret, 7 February 1951. (USN/NARS)

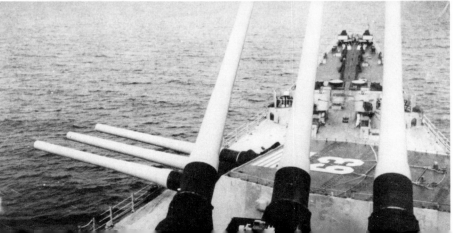

A huge floating drydock, AFDB-1, was towed to Orote, Guam, to provide a forward repair facility for the Iowas, should such become necessary. Wisconsin was used as a guinea pig in a flotation test conducted during April 1952. The bulbous underwater bow that characterized all US fast battleships can be plainly seen. (USN)

(Above Left) Wisconsin fires a salvo off the Korean coast during 1952. She still retains much of here WWII radar suite, including Mk 12/22 antennas on her Mk 37 directors, Mk 13 fire control radars on her main battery directors and an SC air search set aft. The SPS-6 air search antenna on her foremast is new. (Jerry Goldstein)

By late 1952 the commitment of fast battleships off Korea was coming to an end and the Iowas' days of active service were again numbered. Here Iowa is seen off Pearl Harbor, 28 October 1952. Note the hull number and flag markings, now larger and carried on both her forward turrets. (USN)

After the Korean War, the Iowas served for several years before being retired to the reserves. During this period they were given another major refit and emerged with further reduced AA fits and a much upgraded radar suite. Wisconsin has lost two pairs of quad 40mm mounts and the last of her Oerlikons and now mounts a completely new radar outfit (except for the Mk 13s still on her main battery directors). Identifiable radars include Mk 25 dishes on her Mk 37 directors and SPS-10 sea search and SPS-12 air search antennas on her foremast. Note also the deletion of all aircraft handling equipment from her fantail. (USN)

(Above and Below) During maneuvers in dense fog off Cape Henry, Wisconsin and the destroyer escort Eaton crossed paths, with the sad results evidenced by these photos, May 1956. Wisconsin wasn't seriously damaged, but Eaton had to be towed stern first into port. Not too long after the collision, Wisconsin followed her sisters into mothballs. (Jerry Goldstein)

This time the budget-cutters caught up with Missouri, which had avoided being laid up after WWII. Between 1957 and 1967, the US Navy had no battleships in active service. During this period all six North Carolinas and South Dakotas were scrapped. Had the Vietnam War not intervened in the late 1960s, the same fate would probably have overtaken the Iowas. Missouri is seen in mothballs at Bremerton, WA, in September 1976. (USN)

Aircraft

All of the fast battleships were intended to carry catapult-launched floatplanes for spotting work. All were completed with a catapult on either side of the fantail and an aircraft handling crane right aft. Only rarely would these aircraft have an opportunity to actually perform the service for which they were intended. Incidents such as the engagement of Jean Bart by Massachusetts at Casablanca, during which one of the battleships' OS2U Kingfishers placidly circled the target reporting the fall of shot, were so rare as to be virtually unique. The rapid growth of naval aviation made the use of slow floatplanes nearly suicidal in combat situations and the equally rapid improvement in shipborne fire-control radars made their use as spotters superfluous. Generally, the use of shipboard floatplanes was restricted to non-combat functions, such as search and rescue or liaison.

The standard scout aircraft carried by US fast battleships during most of WWII was the Vought OS2U Kingfisher. Three was the normal complement, one for each catapult and a spare. Toward the end of the war, the smaller and faster Curtiss SC-1 Seahawk began to replace Kingfishers.

(Above Left) The US Navy's standard shipboard, catapult launched floatplane for most of WWII was the Vought OS2U Kingfisher, such as the single example seen here on Iowa's fantail, May 1943. In order to handle fixed wing aircraft, battleships needed the various pieces of equipment seen here, including one or more massive catapults and the large aircraft handling crane. (USN/NARS)

(Left) Late in WWII, Kingfishers began to give way to a faster single-place scout, the Curtiss SC-1 Seahawk. This pair of Seahawks are seen on Iowa's fantail in July of 1947. Like all naval aircraft of the era, these two are finished in overall Gloss Sea Blue and carry their unit codes on their tails in large white letters. 'BA' stood for VPMS-7, the battleship scout squadron. (USN/NHC)

(Below) Inevitably, fixed wing aircraft gave way to rotary wing since helicopters were ideally suited to operate from the restricted space on a battleship's fantail, required much less ancillary equipment and were less affected by rough water. Iowa is seen off Wonsan, Korea, on 18 April 1952 carrying the Navy's earliest production helicopter, a Sikorsky HO3S-1 Dragonfly. It carries the markings 'UP-27', indicating it is the 27th aircraft of HU-1, the Navy's first seagoing helicopter squadron. Iowa's catapults have been removed, but for the moment she still retains her aircraft handling crane. (USN/NARS)

The storage of fueled and often armed aircraft in an unprotected position on the deck caused proper concern. This was borne out during the Second Naval Battle of Guadalcanal. Muzzle blast from South Dakota's number three turret set two of her OS2Us afire at the beginning of the engagement. Fortunately, the next salvo blew the burning aircraft overboard and put out most of the fires. No solution to this problem was ever adopted by the US Navy. The Japanese addressed it in their Yamatos which stored their scout aircraft in a hangar under the fantail.

With the role of shipboard aircraft largely restricted to rescue operations in the postwar world, it was only natural that helicopters would replace floatplanes as soon as the type proved reliable. Soon after the end of World War II, the Iowas had their catapults removed and eventually the aircraft handling crane as well. During their Korean War deployment, the Iowas carried a single Sikorsky HO3S-1 belonging to either HU-1 or HU-2, the two original naval helicopter units formed on 1 April 1947. Helicopter evolution was rapid and the Sikorskys were replaced by the bigger, more capable Piaseki HUP. During New Jersey's Vietnam deployment no aircraft were stationed onboard, although her fantail was capable of landing even the largest helicopters and was often used for that purpose. In their current configuration, the Iowas are intended to deploy a single Sikorsky SH-60B Seahawk LAMPS III helicopter. For the first time, dedicated helicopter handling facilities are provided, including a control station, special tie-down positions and lead-in winches, JP-5 tanks for refueling and a glideslope indicator.

(Above) It is intended that New Jersey and the rest of the recommissioned Iowas be capable of operating the Navy's new LAMPS III aircraft, the Sikorsky SH-60B Seahawk, the first production example of which was delivered to the Navy in August 1983. It remains to be seen whether LAMPS will be permanently assigned to the Iowas. (Sikorsky)

(Above Left) The Dragonfly's primary replacement was the Piasecki HUP Retriever. This HUP-2 of HU-2 ('UR' tailcode) prepares to land on Wisconsin's fantail in February of 1956. (Jerry Goldstein)

(Left) For much of the past two decades, various marks of the Sikorsky H-3 Sea King have been the Navy's standard shipborne helicopter. As such it was proper that an SH-3A should have the honor of making the first landing on the rebuilt New Jersey during her initial sea trials in 1982. HU-1 has changed its designation to HC-1, but the tailcode remains 'UP'. (USN)

New Jersey Again....

The Vietnam War proved, among other things, that tactical airpower is an expensive way to project conventional munitions. It occurred to some bright souls in the Pentagon that a much more effective means of firepower delivery existed for targets within the coastal zone (which in case of Vietnam included approximately 80 percent of the potential targets). A rush order went to the Philadelphia Naval Yard, directing that New Jersey be refitted for service off the coast of Vietnam. Seen over the bows of the moth-balled Wisconsin and Iowa, New Jersey is being hastily overhauled, 26 February 1968. (USN)

New Jersey's primary radars are the same that she carried a decade earlier, SPS-10 and SPS-12 on her foremast and WWII-vintage Mk 13 fire control radars on her main battery directors. Light and medium AA guns have entirely disappeared. Markings for a helipad have been applied to New Jersy's fantail but she still retains her large aircraft handling crane, August 1968. (USN)

Emerging from the Philadelphia yard, New Jersey heads out to sea for her third set of sea trials. She now sports a modern conical-monopole antenna at her bow and extensive modifications to her upper tower structure to carry the much enhanced ECM and communications equipment, 25 March 1968. (USN)

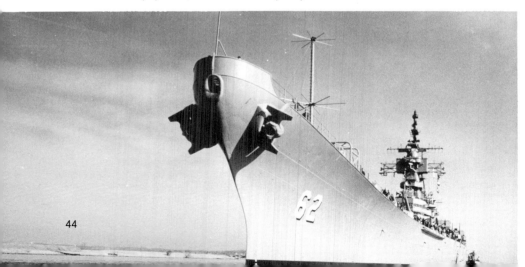

New Jersey spent 120 days actually on the 'firing line' off the coast of Vietnam, during which she fired 5688 rounds of 16' ordnance. (In comparison, during WWII she fired a total of 771 main battery rounds.) (USN)

A full nine gun salvo is a rare event in the life of a battleship, a luxury indulged in only to please photographers. The strain placed on the ship's structure by firing all nine guns is enormous and is generally avoided. Still, this photo does make a point about the ability of a battleship to deliver destruction. Firing full salvoes, New Jersey can deliver 210 tons of ordnance to a target in nine minutes. A single aircraft carrier needs approximately twelve hours to do the same job. (USN)

And Again....

New Jersey was retired again in 1969, for what appeared to be a final rest before being consigned to the cutter's torch. Were it not for the persistence of Charles Myers and other civilian and military battleship supporters such might indeed have been their fate, but the arguments in favor of reactivating the Iowas finally were so persuasive that New Jersey's resurrection was approved by Congress in 1980.

(Above Left) In July of 1981, New Jersey was eased out her berth at Bremerton, WA, where she had been mothballed for twelve years. (USN)

(Above) One civilian tug and two Navy fleet tugs were required to haul New Jersey from Bremerton to Long Beach, CA, where her modernization was to take place. (USN)

(Left) Once at Long Beach, the first order of business was a thorough inspection and cleaning of her undersides. At the same time, work began on reshaping her superstructure to hold new weapons and sensors. (USN)

(Below) Refloated again, scafolds now cover nearly all of New Jersey's upper surfaces as work proceeds rapidly. Note the disappearance of the large open structures previously carried on either side of her upper tower mast. (USN)

New Jersey at sea under her own power again for the first time in a dozen years during mid 1982. A number of her new weapons and sensors can be seen in this view. On each of her tower mast 'wings' she carries an SLQ-32 ESM fixed dielectric lens antenna. At the same level as her Mk 37 directors (with their late 1940s vintage Mk 25 radars), two of New Jersey's four new CIWS Phalanx 20mm rotary cannons for anti-ship missile defense can be seen. (USN)

New Jersey firing her guns on her second sea trial, 20 October 1982. The gun tubs that once held her quad 40mm mounts have been removed, as have two pairs of her twin 5" turrets and her main mast, giving her a very bare appearance. At this time, the fitting of her new weapons was incomplete. Only one of four Tomahawk cruise missile armored box launchers to be mounted on the platform between her funnels is in place and neither of another pair intended to flank her aft tower on either side is visible. Two four-missile Harpoon anti-ship cruise missile launchers can be seen at the base of her after funnel. (USN)

The new cooler burning powder adopted for New Jersey's Vietnam deployment uses a large single powder case compared to the smaller, silk-bagged charges used during WWII. These crewmen gently maneuver a 655lb powder casing toward the powder magazine. (USN)

New Weapons

Harpoon

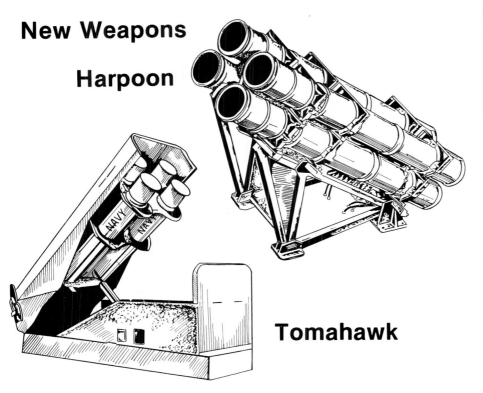

Tomahawk

One of New Jersey's four Phalanx CIWSs is test fired. The 20mm rotary cannon ('Gatling Gun') fires a depleted-uranium shot at a rate of 3000rpm, providing close-in defense against anti-ship missiles. (USN)

Iowa arriving at Litton-Ingalls Shipbuilding facility at Pascagoula, MS, on 30 January 1983. Much more work will be involved in modernizing Iowa than New Jersey because Iowa hasn't been in service since 1953. All of her 5" turrets and all fire control directors were removed as part of the mothballing process and now must be refitted. (USN)

Iowa is being eased out of Philadelphia Naval Ship Yard prior to beginning the long journey to New Orleans and her first overhaul in 30 years. She arrived at Avondale Shipyards on 15 September, where all hull work and ripout was done. (USN)

A proud, gray lady sails again! New Jersey was commissioned at Long Beach on 28 December 1982 by President Ronald Reagan. Her first active duty assignment came in August of 1983 when she and her accompanying destroyers were sent to the waters of the Pacific off Nicaragua to demonstrate US power in Central America. Perhaps no first mission could have been more ironic than that. The first 'modern' battleships emerged in the late 19th century as a means of projecting a nation's power. Often the arrival of a battleship or two off an unfriendly shore was enough to calm a troubled situation. Once again she is the right ship at the right time, some 40 years after her birth. (USN)

New Jersey leads six smaller ships comprising its Surface Action Group on maneuvers off California, 15 April 1983. After a brief deployment off Nicaragua in August, New Jersey headed for the Mediterranean and Lebanon in mid-September, 1983. (USN)